Gertrude Chandler Warner

* * * * * * * * * * * * * * * * * * *

and *The Boxcar Children*

Mary Ellen Ellsworth

illustrated by Marie DeJohn

Albert Whitman & Company
Morton Grove, Illinois

Library of Congress Cataloging-in-Publication Data

Ellsworth, Mary Ellen.
Gertrude Chandler Warner and *The Boxcar Children* / written by Mary Ellen Ellsworth;
illustrated by Marie DeJohn.
p.   cm.

Summary: A biography of the woman who created the well-known stories about the adventures of
four children who lived in a railroad car until going to stay with their grandfather.

ISBN 0-8075-2837-4 (hardcover)
ISBN 0-8075-2838-2 (paperback)
1. Warner, Gertrude Chandler, 1890– Juvenile literature.   2. Warner, Gertrude Chandler, 1890–
Boxcar children – Juvenile literature.   3. Women authors, American – 20th century – Biography–
Juvenile literature.   4. Children's stories – Authorship – Juvenile literature.   [1. Warner, Gertrude
Chandler, 1890–.   2. Authors, American.   3. Women – Biography.]   I. DeJohn, Marie, ill.   II. Title.

PS3545.A738Z65   1997   96-32814
813'.52 – dc20
                                                                                        CIP
[B]   AC

Text copyright © 1997 by Mary Ellen Ellsworth.
Illustrations copyright © 1997 by Marie DeJohn.
Published in 1997 by Albert Whitman & Company,
6340 Oakton Street, Morton Grove, Illinois 60053.
Published simultaneously in Canada by
General Publishing, Limited, Toronto.
Printed in the United States of America.
10 9 8 7 6 5 4

The text of this book is set in Oldstyle.
Design by Scott Piehl.

For more information about Albert Whitman & Company,
please visit our website at www.albertwhitman.com.

To my mother, Marguerite Tressel.
To my husband, Mike.
And to our children, Rob, Pat, Liz, and Kathleen,
who have all been readers of the Boxcar series.

Contents

Chapter One

Growing Up On Main Street

WHEN GERTRUDE CHANDLER WARNER was little, she lived in a house right across the street from a railroad station. She liked to look into the caboose of the train that stopped there. Inside she could see a small stove with a tin coffeepot on it. On a little table there were cracked cups with no saucers. What fun, she thought, to keep house in a caboose!

The Warner family lived in Putnam, Connecticut, a town surrounded by the rolling hills, tall woods, and many rivers of the New England countryside. Gertrude spent all of her life there. The town had been named for General Israel Putnam, who led troops in the Revolutionary War.

Gertrude's mother's and father's families had lived in eastern Connecticut for a long time. Her father, Judge Edgar Warner, was a descendant of Ichabod Warner, one of the early settlers of Windham County, and of John Avery of Groton, who fought in the Revolutionary War. Her mother, Jane Elizabeth Carpenter Warner, was a descendant of the Chandlers, who had come to nearby Woodstock, Connecticut, in 1686, ninety years before the American Revolution.

Edgar Warner graduated from Harvard Law School in 1872. In 1885, he opened a law office in Putnam, and two years later he and Jane Elizabeth Carpenter married. Edgar and Jane Warner were helpful people who became involved in the everyday life of Putnam. Edgar became the first judge of the city court; and Jane, or Jennie, as she was called, became head of the town school committee.

Gertrude Chandler Warner was born on April 16, 1890. She was the middle of three children. Her sister, Frances, was two years older; and her brother, John, was two years younger. The children grew up in the house at 42 South Main Street, which had been built for their family by Gertrude's grandfather, John Carpenter. During Gertrude's childhood, the house was heated by wood and lit by kerosene lamps.

The children were very much at the center of the family's life. One time when carpenters came to add a fireplace to the house, when Gertrude was about three, they also lowered some of the house windows so that Gertrude and Frances and John could look out without having to climb up on a chair or a window seat. Frances later said that they had little to complain about. Once though, on a winter afternoon, she and Gertrude did plan to run away because their mother made them stop sliding down the icy back porch roof!

Gertrude was a busy and active young girl, but she was not very strong. She had a lot of sore throats. There were few vaccines then, so she also got many childhood illnesses such as measles and mumps. Still, she attended the Fifth District School House with the other Putnam children.

Gertrude loved to read. She often went to the public library, which was on the second floor of a building near the Warners' home. Gertrude would take a book out on a Saturday morning, read it, and return it that afternoon. She was disappointed when the librarian, Miss Emma Kinney, told her she could not take out another book that same day. She had to wait until the next time the library opened—and that wasn't until Wednesday! Her favorite book was *Alice's Adventures in Wonderland.*

Gertrude and Frances wrote their own stories and poems. Their mother always bought notebooks for them so they could be neat and organized. But sometimes Gertrude had trouble finding a good pencil around the house. She always said her family had the worst old pencil stubs—they had to be sharpened with a kitchen knife!

Gertrude wrote her first book when she was just nine years old. She had been late getting home from school several days in a row, and her mother wanted to know why. She told her mother she was writing a "Golliwogg Book." But she really had been having tea parties on the flat rock in the schoolyard. When her mother wanted to see the book, Gertrude had to write it fast! She called her book *Golliwogg at the Zoo*, copying the idea of Florence Upton's popular 1898 book, *The Golliwogg at the Sea-Side*. Gertrude illustrated the book with watercolors and gave it to Grandfather Carpenter for Christmas in 1900. The book plate at the front of the book says: "Mr. John A. Carpenter, Compliments of Authoress and Illustrator." After that, Gertrude made a new book each Christmas.

The next year Gertrude's book contained three short stories: "Two Christmases," "The Mumps," and "13230 Gold Dollars." She gave this one to Grandmother Carpenter. In 1902 she wrote "A Fish Story," which Frances illustrated. The girls listed the publisher of their book as "Warner & Co." Two years later, "A Thanksgiving Story" was "composed and type-written by Gertrude and bound by Frances." In 1906, Gertrude put together photos and typed the story for "Reminiscences of an Old Farm," which she "lovingly dedicated to Grandpa" at Christmas time.

Gertrude enjoyed playing with her dollhouse, which had handmade furniture and china dolls about the length of her hand. Mr. and Mrs. Delight were the doll family, and Gertrude was the carpenter who made new furniture for them, the dressmaker who clothed them, and the doctor who talked to them about their "medicines." Sometimes Gertrude tried to make special items for the house. To make a pretend pair of scissors, she once put pins on the nearby railroad track. She thought that the trains passing over would push the pins together just enough to make a perfect pair of tiny scissors. But the engine was so heavy it ground the pins to nothing. Gertrude found that the trolley track worked better for her experiment. At last the dollhouse got a decent pair of scissors.

There was always work as well as play at the Warners' house. The family lived so near the railroad tracks that smoke and cinders from the trains covered the house's windowsills. The sills had to be dusted twice every day, and the curtains needed to be washed often.

Gertrude earned some money by killing the flies in the house. The Warners lived right by a road where horse-drawn buggies often passed—and that meant flies. Gertrude got ten cents for every hundred she killed. She always found it easy to get a hundred.

Sometimes Gertrude and her family planned picnics in the Connecticut hills of Woodstock and Pomfret and clambakes in nearby Rhode Island. When Gertrude was seven, the whole family went to the beach for the first time. The children had never seen the ocean. Gertrude loved the beautiful white sand of the shore and the fancy meals they had at their summer cottage. She called the family's vacation at the beach "seventh heaven!"

Gertrude began taking wonderful Sunday afternoon rides with her Grandfather Carpenter when she was eight. He would call to ask, "Want to go to the farm?" The answer was always, "Yes!" Soon a two-seated buggy pulled by a little black horse named Topsy came to the door, and the whole family piled in. The children took turns sitting in the front seat beside Grandpa, and sometimes they even got to drive. That is how Gertrude learned to drive a horse.

The children knew that the Carpenters' farmhouse, built in 1803 and owned by Gertrude's Great-Uncle Charles, was exactly two and three-quarters miles down River Road. They had measured the distance themselves. They tied a rag to a spoke of the wheel and then counted how many times the wheel went around between their house and the farm. When they

multiplied the number of revolutions by the circumference of the wheel, they knew the exact distance!

On the ride, they passed a pond which was filled with peep-frogs and wild blue flag flowers in the spring. Sometimes they stopped at the edge of a bog. Once, at the risk of their lives, Gertrude thought, they climbed over the stone wall along the side of the bog to search for blue iris for an herbarium Frances was making.

They often stopped at a watering trough to give Topsy a drink. Then they all drank out of the rusty tin dipper there. Nearby, they picked flowers—violets in spring, goldenrod and asters in late summer. Gertrude liked the violets best of all. Soon she and the other children knew the names of every wildflower around. Gertrude learned to recognize all the birds and their songs, too.

When the children arrived at the Carpenter farm, they each got one of Aunt Lyddy's sugar cookies, made in the shape of an oak leaf, from her special covered tin pail. They ate their cookies slowly, breaking off one section of the leaf at a time. Then they went for a walk.

In the woods near the farmhouse they sometimes found treasures. In spring they found "pippins," or young, tender checkerberry leaves, to nibble. Once they found a rare flower, the giant purple fringed orchis. It was six feet tall!

If they went toward the spring, they passed the hay barns, the pigpen, and the chicken house, where the hens were sitting on newly laid eggs. They went by the cranberry bog and sometimes picked the sour cranberries. Along the brook they found watercress. The peppery watercress, mixed into a boiled dressing, made a good salad.

Sometimes they went over to the pond and climbed into the two flat-bottomed boats tied up there. They would row around the pond, trailing their fingers in the warm water and watching the darting fish.

But for excitement nothing could beat watching the trains that went right by the Warners' house. Many trains passed, day and night. At least four a day went to New York City. The train everyone called the "White Train," because it was painted all white and gold, went through Putnam on its way to New York about 4:00 P.M. The children waved to the people on the White Train, and the engineer and passengers waved back.

Many trains also went to Boston and Worcester, Massachusetts. Trains from the south always blew a loud whistle just before they entered the "cut," a steep-sided valley cut through the rocks. The trains brought mail to Putnam several times a day. Sometimes the Warners and other townspeople took a train for a day of shopping in one of the nearby cities.

The children, especially Gertrude, also liked to look into the

railroad station across the street. It had a large dining room, where tables were set with damask cloths and napkins and railroad silverware. Putnam was an important railroad center in the early 1900s, and travelers changing rail lines could be fed well at the station.

There were a lot of different shops in Putnam, not far from the Warners' home. When Gertrude was a little older, she did errands for her family. At Champeau's Dry Goods Shop, when a customer paid for something, the money was put in a cup and sent along wires to a cage in the back of the shop. There the store owner made change, which was put back into the cup and returned along the wire to the counter where customers waited. Gertrude thought this was magic!

Gertrude also went to Pray's Market with her family. They had to go down a flight of stone steps into the market, and it always felt so damp there that Gertrude wondered why everyone didn't catch cold.

She and her family bought red disks of Edam cheese, large pickles, salt pork for baked beans, and in the cold season, roast pork. If Gertrude needed patterns for sewing, she went to Manning's Dry Goods Store and got them from Miss Lottie Manning.

Sometimes when Gertrude went off to the shops on her own, she got lost. She did not know Union Square from Union Street.

Somehow, though, she used to find her way to Payne's Candy Store to buy stick candy. Gertrude liked the talking parrot there. She always asked him questions, but he didn't answer them very often!

When Gertrude and Frances were in grade school, they had a theater and a symphony in the attic, with a broken melodeon as the main instrument. Everyone in Gertrude's family enjoyed music. When Gertrude was a teenager, she became fascinated with the cello. One day her father came home from New York City with a cello for her. The cello, a bow, a carrying case, and an instruction book cost fourteen dollars. That was about the price of a new bicycle then. It was also about two weeks of a teacher's salary. Her father had brought her a special gift!

Gertrude's family soon formed a home orchestra. Gertrude played the cello, Frances and Mother played violins, Papa was on piano, and John played the coronet. They had wonderful times playing together, and sometimes friends joined in.

When Gertrude was halfway through her second year of high school, she had to stop going to classes. She was having terrible sore throats, and was coughing and sneezing a lot. Instead of going to school, she studied at home with a tutor, and her mother taught her lessons, too. Frances finished high school in 1907, and John finished in 1912. Gertrude never did graduate, though she continued with her home lessons.

In 1907, Grandfather Carpenter died. His death ended a chapter in the children's lives. Frances wrote that Grandmother often said Grandfather's "favorite recreation" was his grandchildren. In her 1904 "A Thanksgiving Story," Gertrude had written about the laughter and play, talk, and good food the family shared when they gathered at Grandfather and Grandmother Carpenter's home. They all "felt as much at home there as in their own houses," she said. Grandma "had the basket of toys and the high-chairs, the little knives and forks, and the ginger-cookies; and Grandpa was always ready to play."

Chapter Two

Creating A Life

I N THE EARLY 1900S, Putnam was growing. New
schools and churches were built. New bridges were
constructed over the rivers, using cement rather than
wood as in the past.

Life was becoming easier and more comfortable in Putnam.
At the turn of the century, a local paper called the *Putnam
Patriot* advertised water- and steam-heating systems, refriger-
ators, and gas stoves for people's homes. Local stores offered
treadle sewing machines, bicycles, pianos and parlor organs,
and cameras for their customers' use and pleasure. By 1906
and 1907, automobiles and typewriters were for sale. Edison

phonographs and records, and safety razors, too, could be purchased by Putnam shoppers. The local power company advertised, "We will not be Satisfied till every house in the City is equipped with Electricity and Gas for Lighting."

The most exciting invention, though, was the automobile. The first one Gertrude ever saw was a steam-powered car called the Stanley Steamer. It was driven by a man named Carl Hopkins. Whenever he drove by, everyone rushed out to look.

In 1905 moving pictures could be viewed at the local Bradley Playhouse. Dramas and minstrel shows were performed, too. *Isle of Spice*, a Broadway show with twenty whistling songs and unique dances, came to Putnam on November 27, 1905.

There were changes in the Warner household, too, as the children began to pursue new opportunities. In 1911, Frances graduated from Mount Holyoke College in South Hadley, Massachusetts. She soon began teaching high school. John went on to Worcester Polytechnic Institute, also in Massachusetts, and graduated in 1917. He then went to study in Paris for two years.

Gertrude wondered what she was going to do. She began writing for a Sunday school newspaper published in the nearby town of Danielson. She got one dollar for every five hundred words. She also worked with her mother and sister to put together "A Chandler Book." It told about the ancestors of

Marcia Jane Chandler Carpenter, Gertrude's grandmother, and showed family photographs taken in 1915.

Gertrude wished to have a real book published—one that would be for everybody, not just her family. In 1916, her wish came true. Gertrude had her first officially published book. One thousand copies were printed. *The House of Delight* is about her wonderful childhood dollhouse, where the small china dolls named Mr. and Mrs. Delight lived. Gertrude's brother, John, took the photographs for the book. Their cousin, Bertha Child, posed for the pictures of "Betsey," who is the head of the miniature "house of delight." Gertrude dedicated this book, like the stories she had written as a young child, to Grandfather Carpenter. She called him "my Best playmate." "It was an epoch to have something published," she said.

Gertrude's mother had once told her and Frances that she liked to see them writing but didn't think they could make a career of it. For once their mother was wrong! Gertrude and Frances began publishing stories and essays in magazines. Frances also began teaching English at Mount Holyoke College.

Mrs. Warner had also been wrong about World War I. She thought the world was too advanced for fighting. But the war that had begun in Europe in 1914 continued. There was terrible fighting there, and millions of people died. In 1917, the United States became involved by declaring war on Germany.

Life changed in Putnam, and everywhere else in the United States, too. Some young men left Putnam to go fight overseas. Some of the women helped out by working in the textile mills that made cloth and thread, and by doing other jobs that needed to be done in the war emergency. People put up American flags in front of their homes to show how much they cared about their country. Many people volunteered to help the American Red Cross, which was working to get bandages and supplies to soldiers fighting in faraway countries. Gertrude's grandmother began knitting socks for the fighting men. Gertrude helped the Red Cross with publicity.

By 1918, there were not enough teachers at the local school because so many had left to fight in the war. Even though Gertrude had not gone to college, or even finished high school, she began to teach first grade in the Israel Putnam School— "just for a little while"—until the war shortage ended.

Gertrude began by assisting another teacher for a few hours each day. But there was an influenza epidemic that year, and the other teacher died. Gertrude took over. She had forty children in her morning class and forty in her afternoon class. She said she learned by doing. She had a big job, but she did it very well. Her salary was raised five times during that first year of teaching—from four hundred to one thousand dollars.

Gertrude continued to live at home with her parents, like

many other young women of the time who had not married. She and her mother were good friends. Although her mother was not a writer, she came up with the ideas for almost everything Gertrude wrote. She suggested a nature series, which fit in with Gertrude's love of flowers and birds and stars. Gertrude wrote the series for *Little Folks* magazine. The different stories had pen-and-ink drawings of stars, wildflowers, shells, birds, and butterflies.

Gertrude also played the piano for a boys' club called the Pages of King Arthur. The boys happened to be studying the stars. Gertrude had just learned all the constellations, so she took over the boys' group and taught them astronomy herself!

In 1918 a Boston publisher collected Gertrude's stories about the stars and constellations for a book called *Star Stories for Little Folks*. People wanted to buy it because it was an astronomy book that was easy to understand.

Gertrude and Frances continued writing essays for magazines such as the *Atlantic Monthly* and *Ladies' Home Journal*. In 1921 they published some of their essays in a book called *Life's Minor Collisions*. These essays for grownups are humorous and lively. The writers dedicated the book to Grandmother Carpenter.

In two of the essays, Gertrude writes about her experiences as an elementary school teacher. She talks about the drawer full of children's treasures that a teacher collects. In the drawer might be horse chestnuts, wire twisted into eyeglasses, and "snapping bugs"—the tin noisemakers sold from ice cream trucks for one penny each. The objects often included the maple tree's seed pod—the large, pale green "key" which children knew how to split so that it would stay perched just right on their noses. Once, Gertrude said, one of her students read her the story "The Three Billy Goats Gruff" while he had one maple key over each ear, one on his nose, and two on his cheeks. She admits she was more interested in the balancing of the maple keys than in the story!

"The Return of A, B, C" tells how Gertrude began to use the sounds of letters, or phonics, instead of letters' names, to teach first graders to read. For W, for example, she found it was much more useful for a child "to pucker up his lips like the howling wind" than to label it "Double-you."

Even as a teacher, Gertrude sometimes got sick and had to miss school. Her writing got done more quickly when she was forced to stay at home, though. That quiet time allowed her to concentrate. In 1924 she had just finished eight books for a religious organization. She was home with bronchitis, and while she was resting she thought about what kind of book she wanted to write just to suit herself. She thought about a different kind of life—about living on her own in a freight car or caboose. She imagined four children doing just that. *The Boxcar Children* was the result. It was published with beautiful illustrations by Dorothy Lake Gregory. Gertrude later said the book "raised a storm of protest from librarians, who thought the children were having too good a time without any parental control!" She added, "That is exactly why children like it!"

During 1924 Gertrude also learned to play the pipe organ so she could accompany the choir at the Congregational church. She would leave school and practice until suppertime. Then she practiced for two hours after supper. On Saturdays she practiced all day, stopping just for meals. Her mother finally rationed her, and said she could practice only nine hours on Saturday! Gertrude was substituting for the regular organist, who was away for six weeks, and she didn't want to make any mistakes.

In 1926 Gertrude published her book *Good Americans: First Lessons in Citizenship; First Lessons for the Littlest Ones.* But through all these years, her main focus was teaching in the Israel Putnam School. She turned out to be a wonderful teacher. Instead of just filling in during the war years, she ended up teaching first grade and sometimes third grade for the next thirty-two years.

Gertrude was a good teacher for many reasons. She knew

that every girl and boy in her classes was special, and she found a way to remind each child of that. She also respected each child. She said, "[I know the children] are beneath me only in years."

Gertrude loved the natural world. She raised beautiful gardens, with flowers—zinnias and hollyhocks and petunias—and with vegetables like tomatoes, parsnips, and carrots. She pressed wildflowers and made collections of butterflies and moths. It is no wonder that her students grew to love the outdoor world, too.

Every year the children in her class had a contest to see who could collect the most different kinds of wildflowers. The first one in the class to find a flower got the credit for it. If two or more children found a certain flower on the same day, each one got credit. But no one could get credit for that same flower a day or two later! No one would tell the secret hiding places of the special flowers, either.

One year, someone brought in a flower that had grown near a patch of poison ivy, but no one knew that. Gertrude got covered with poison ivy rash, and the children had a substitute teacher for a while.

When Gertrude taught third grade, the children grew string beans in pots on the classroom windowsills. Gertrude took the plants home on weekends to make sure they got watered. The class harvested the beans and cooked them over a Bunsen burner. The children had fun, and they learned a lot about sharing: one year there were thirty children in the class and only about twelve beans! But everyone had a bite.

On rainy days, Gertrude brought out Happy, a clown puppet, from the corner of the classroom. Happy the Clown answered the children's questions. If a child were quiet or shy, Gertrude would make Happy say, "Wouldn't you like to ask a question?" Pretty soon, the child was taking part.

She also made a paper doll, Billy Bump, who dressed for the weather. On a showery day, for example, he wore a raincoat. Billy always brushed his teeth and combed his hair. He taught Gertrude's young students about good health and cleanliness.

Gertrude found ways to celebrate special days for each student. She sent birthday cards to the children, and tied birthday bows on the backs of their chairs. She had a wooden cake painted to look real, with holes for candles drilled in the top. After the candles were lit, the class sang "Happy Birthday" and applauded.

The birthday child wore a "bluebird of happiness" sticker for the rest of the day. If a girl or boy had a summer birthday, Gertrude would find a day during the school year when no one else had a birthday and make that day the one to celebrate for the summer child.

Gertrude could draw well, too, and she did pictures for the schoolroom. She sometimes drew the Wolf Den, a nearby natural cave, on the first-grade blackboard. While she was drawing the picture, Gertrude told the children the history of the Wolf Den. In the winter of 1742–1743, Israel Putnam, then a young farmer, awoke one morning to find seventy of his sheep and goats dead. They had been attacked during the night by an old wolf who had raided animal flocks in the area for years. Since she had lost two of her toes in a trap, her tracks identified her at once. A group of farmers tracked the wolf all day and all night. At last she went to her den. They watched again all day and tried to force her out of hiding. Finally, when everything else had failed, Israel Putnam went into the den alone. Just as the wolf started to attack him, he raised his gun and shot her. Then he brought her carcass out for everyone to see. The picture of the wolf den and the story that went with it certainly captured the children's imaginations!

Gertrude made a silhouette of each of her first-grade students for the child to keep. Silhouettes are outline drawings, filled in with black. They look like shadows and are usually done in profile. Here is a silhouette Gertrude did for Ruth Erickson, one of her first graders, more than fifty years ago.

Gertrude also decorated fancy hand-blown Easter eggs for every girl and boy in her class. Each blue, yellow, or pink egg was trimmed with a ribbon and had the child's name written in gold.

Gertrude shared her love of music with her first graders. The children had a marching band. They played cymbals, flutes, drums, harmonicas, blocks, triangles, bells, tambourines, and tin whistles. The band leader wore a uniform, and the band played for all flag salutes, birthdays, and other special occasions.

On May Day, the first day of May, the school flagpole became the Maypole, with brightly colored ribbons wound around it by the children. Somehow the children and the ribbons never got tangled up.

The celebrations and gifts made each child feel loved and valued. Gertrude Chandler Warner's classroom in the Israel Putnam School was a wonderful place to be.

Gertrude Chandler Warner, age 10

Gertrude Chandler Warner and her first-grade students at Israel Putnam School, 1924

John A. C. Warner, 1905

John A. C. Warner's radio tower at 42 South Main

QUINEBAUG RIVER

Bird's-eye view of Putnam, 1887

Fifth District School, Putnam, 1890s

Railroad crossing, Putnam, 1890s

Flood of 1955, Putnam

Quinebaug River, aerial view of flood of 1955

Woman's Union of the Congregational Church in Putnam.
First woman standing at left: Esther Welles.
Third woman from left, standing: Gertrude Chandler Warner.

The Carpenter family, 1907.
Back row: Will Carpenter, Mame Carpenter, Edgar Warner,
Gertrude Chandler Warner, Alice Carpenter, Fred Carpenter, Frances Warner, Chester Child.
Middle row: Jennie Carpenter Warner, John Carpenter, Marcia Jane Carpenter, Annie Carpenter Child.
Front row: John Warner, Maud Carpenter, Mary Carpenter, Ruth Child, Pauline Carpenter.

Train on trestle over Quinebaug River, 1890s

Railroad yard, Putnam, 1925

Gertrude Chandler Warner, 1966

Chapter Three

Focusing On Writing

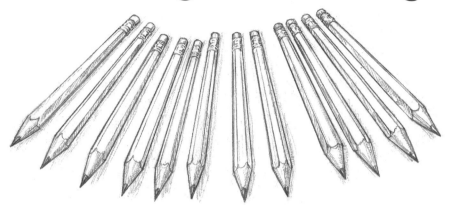

IN 1928, Gertrude's father died at the age of seventy-eight. Edgar Warner had contributed to many parts of Putnam life, and he was greatly missed. After his death, Gertrude and her mother moved a few doors away, to 106 South Main Street, to live with Grandmother Carpenter. Although Marcia Jane Carpenter was an invalid during the last twelve years of her life, she was alert and busy—knitting or talking with her children and grandchildren. The family made sure Grandmother was never left in the house alone; one of the children or grandchildren visited her every day.

Grandma Carpenter died in 1929. Gertrude and her mother continued to live at 106 South Main Street until 1932, when

Mrs. Warner died. Jennie Warner was only sixty-six years old at her death.

Gertrude stayed in the same house, and lived by herself for the first time in her life. Her brother, John, was living in New York. He was now working for the Society of Automotive Engineers, publishing their journal, which told about how cars are put together and how they work. He had married Marion Andem of Putnam in 1920, and they had two sons. Frances, Gertrude's sister, who had been a professor of English at Wellesley College as well as at Mount Holyoke, was now on the staff of the *Atlantic Monthly* magazine. She had married Mayo Hersey in 1922, and was living in Woodbury, New Jersey.

Gertrude, the only member of her family who was unmarried and still at home in Putnam, was very busy teaching and writing. The same qualities that made Gertrude a good teacher—her understanding and sense of humor, her interest in nature, and her joy in day-to-day happenings—also helped make her a good writer of children's stories.

Gertrude wrote four books introducing children of different backgrounds to one another. *The World in a Barn* was published in 1927, *Windows into Alaska* in 1928, *The World on a Farm* in 1931, and *Children of the Harvest* in 1940.

The World in a Barn includes children from Japan, China, the Philippines, and Alaska. Together the children build toy villages representing different parts of the world. *The World on a Farm* tells stories of young people living on farms in the United States and other countries. *Children of the Harvest* is about migrant children who pick fresh fruits and vegetables for the markets. Its goal is to teach other children about migrant workers. Gertrude wrote a letter at the beginning of her book encouraging her readers to write the Home Mission Council in New York City to learn how to send thank-you presents to the working children.

Gertrude and Frances, meanwhile, collected more of their essays which had been in magazines like *House Beautiful* and *Harper's*. In 1933 they published another book for grownups, *Pleasures and Palaces.* Gertrude wrote about playing the pipe organ and visiting her brother in a small New York City apartment. She also wrote about traveling to a Canadian island to get away from the ragweed which caused her hay fever in the early fall. If she traveled alone, Gertrude said, she had a good chance to make a new friend along the way.

Gertrude wrote her part of *Pleasures and Palaces* while she was in a plaster cast, getting over a broken back. On July 20, 1932, she had been in a terrible car accident. Her aunt Annie Child was driving, and turned to miss a truck that was backing up. The car went off the road, hitting two fence posts. Mrs. Child and another passenger were fine, but Gertrude was so seriously injured that she was put on the hospital's danger list. She was in the hospital for four months, and then went to Frances's house in New Jersey for a while afterward. She didn't feel very good, but she had promised to finish the book, and she did. "You can do a lot of things you think you can't," Gertrude said after that. Gertrude and Frances dedicated their book to Dr. Overlook and Dr. Ottenheimer, the two men who had saved Gertrude's life.

During the summer of 1936, Gertrude went to work for a publisher in Chicago, Illinois. She was trying to find ways to write books for children that were both exciting and easy to read.

For the next three summers, Gertrude went to Yale University, one of the most well-known colleges in the United States, to take teacher training courses. She did so well that her teacher thought Gertrude should be a teacher at Yale, not a student. Gertrude had to tell her professor that she had never even finished high school!

Then Gertrude spent another summer working with the publisher in Chicago and living at the YWCA there. She visited stores to try to find children's books with exciting plots that could be rewritten in simple words. She helped develop a new series of easy readers for children who might be having trouble with the usual school reading books.

Over the years, Gertrude had read *The Boxcar Children* to her students many times. She had begun to think about it some more, too. She wanted all children to enjoy it—even those who might be poor readers, and those who might be learning the English language. She wrote a new version which was published in 1942. This is the version that children today have read.

The Boxcar Children is the first story about the four Alden children—Henry, Jessie, Violet, and Benny. They are orphans who live on their own and make their home in an abandoned boxcar. The 1942 version begins: "One warm night four children stood in front of a bakery. No one knew them. No one knew where they had come from."

The words and sentences are easy to understand, and the story is exciting. This is exactly what Gertrude Chandler Warner was trying to achieve. She hoped that children who saw themselves as nonreaders might become hooked. When they found themselves reading and understanding, they would gain confidence and read even more books. This would help them succeed in school and afterward.

Gertrude still remembered her dream of living in a boxcar. She said of *The Boxcar Children*, "It's a very entertaining story, even to me. I would like to have done what they did. I'd still like to do it."

In 1937 Gertrude wrote a biography of Henry Barnard, one of the most important people in the history of American education. She wrote this book for the Connecticut State Teachers' Association. Nine years later, she wrote a history of Connecticut for the same group.

During the 1930s and 1940s, Gertrude continued to be active in the Congregational church of Putnam. In 1948 she wrote the church's history for its one-hundred-year celebration. She also wrote a lot of church skits, for which she designed wonderful costumes. She played the cello and organ for church events, too. And she did the lettering in the Bibles that were presented to the Sunday school children. She was very talented—and busy!

But she never forgot to make other people feel good about their talents and contributions, too. Whenever anything had to be decided, people always said, "Run it by Gertrude; see what she says." She was known for her wisdom, gentleness, and tact. A friend of hers said, "Her words of praise and encouragement could make you feel ten feet tall."

Gertrude somehow found time to write a second Boxcar book. *Surprise Island* was published in 1949. In this story, the Boxcar Children go on an adventure and solve a mystery—just as they do in all the succeeding books.

The following year, at age sixty, Gertrude retired from teaching so she could have more time to write. She said, "I just couldn't wait to be sixty." Over the years she had taught sixteen hundred children! She had loved teaching, but now she wanted to spend as much time as she could writing books—especially books for children.

Gertrude's retirement also gave her more time to pursue her volunteer work. One group she helped was the Connecticut Cancer Society. She was service chairperson in 1950. She felt the

city of Putnam and the people who lived there had been good to her, so she wanted to give back to them.

Gertrude continued to volunteer for the Red Cross, too. She had helped them with publicity as early as 1917, even before she began teaching. She continued to assist the Red Cross over the years, and now she was helping her good friend Esther Welles, who was a community nurse. During the 1955 flood in Putnam, there was a heavy burden of work to do. On August 19, 1955, hurricane winds and rain hit. Two of the city's rivers overflowed and came together, spilling out like a lake and destroying Putnam's three bridges. The city was without electricity, water, telephone, and sewers. More than fifty homes were shattered.

Volunteers were needed to aid flood victims. They helped find food, clothing, and furniture for people who had lost everything in the rushing waters. Sometimes they stayed up all night to get the job done. Everyone helped out, and people soon began to put their lives back together. Gertrude was the one who wrote the reports on the Red Cross role in the disaster for the local newspapers, the *Putnam Patriot* and the *Windham County Observer.*

Gertrude did use most of her time for writing, as she had hoped to. In 1954 she had published a children's book which was not part of the Boxcar series. *1001 Nights* adapts the original *1001 Nights*, often called *The Arabian Nights*, to an easy-reading format. Her third Boxcar story, *The Yellow House Mystery*, had been published the year before, in 1953, and *Mystery Ranch*, the fourth, came out in 1958. The next Boxcar book, *Mike's Mystery*, was due to the publisher in November 1959. In October, Gertrude fell and broke her hip socket. In spite of hospitalization and physical therapy, she met her deadline!

Gertrude's readers loved her books, and they wrote to her, asking for more. One of the things children enjoy most about the Boxcar Children books is that they form a series. Readers meet four children they know and like—Henry, Jessie, Violet, and Benny—and they have the chance to meet them again and again in story after story. They become like good friends. Gertrude kept that relationship going. She published twelve books in twelve years between 1960 and 1971. She dedicated her 1962 *The Woodshed Mystery* "To all readers everywhere, including Guam, who have written to me about the Boxcar Children."

Gertrude first wrote her stories in pencil on the right half of her blank book. When she got to the end, she turned the blank book upside down and wrote on the other side. She started with one dozen soft pencils, all sharpened. She said, "When a pencil gets hot and 'tired' I change to a new one." Sometimes she wrote with pens instead. But whether she wrote in pencil or pen, she saved everything—notes and bits of conversation—in her notebooks. She said, "Never despise a small beginning." She knew that an idea for a whole book could come out of one of those brief notes. Another time she said, "Never throw away what you write. You may want it later." She usually wrote her books at least four times, to make them say just what she wanted.

Gertrude wrote nineteen Boxcar mysteries in all. She always found it great fun to think of a new plot and then to sit down in her home workroom to write it. Her workroom was outfitted with an easy chair, a paper cutter, and a typewriter—although she was not a very good typist! The wallpaper in her workroom was patterned with her favorite flower, the violet, and she often had bunches of violets around the room for decoration.

Chapter Four

Enjoying Community

G ERTRUDE CHANDLER WARNER never married and had a family of her own. She once said, "My brother married my best friend, and my sister married my brother's best friend. Nobody seemed to be available for me, but I have managed to get along very well as a spinster— I suppose because I have had so many things to do." In many ways, her schoolchildren, her readers, and the people of her hometown became her family. In the later part of her life, beginning in 1962, she lived in a brown shingled house on Ring Street with her friend Esther Welles, "surrounded by woods and good neighbors." Sometimes she called this house "the acorn."

In 1965 Gertrude received the Woman of the Year Award from the Emblem Club, a women's group serving the local community. Then in 1967 she received an award for fifty years of service to the American National Red Cross. The respect for individuals that Gertrude showed in her classroom and in her writing also marked the volunteer work she did for the people of Putnam. She cared about them, and she worked hard for them.

Gertrude was often "given back to," as she deserved to be. On one memorable occasion, she was invited by her friend Andrew Donovan, a retired engineer and road foreman, to ride inside a caboose just as she had dreamed of doing for so long. She rode on the back platform. She also ran the diesel engine, blew the whistle, and rang the bell. Gertrude and the road crew shared coffee. "It was more of a thrill, I think, going in after all those years of wishing," she said.

In 1967 Gertrude published *Houseboat Mystery*, another Boxcar book. That same year, she also wrote a different kind of book—*Peter Piper, Missionary Parakeet*—with Lelia Anderson. Reverend Anderson was a missionary who traveled all over the United States with her talkative parakeet. Peter knew eight hundred words, and he could say sentences. The book is based on the friendship the minister and the parakeet shared for ten years and two hundred thousand miles of traveling.

Gertrude continued writing Boxcar books. She wrote *Mystery Behind the Wall* in 1973 and *Bus Station Mystery* in 1974. *Benny Uncovers a Mystery*, her last Boxcar story, came out in 1976.

The imaginary town of Greenfield, where the Boxcar Children live, has many similarities to Putnam. Some say that Benny Alden is based on the young man who used to bring Gertrude new writing pens from the stationery shop when she needed them.

During these busy years, both Gertrude and Esther Welles were frequent visitors to the Putnam Public Library, and they often borrowed books. So at holiday time they made cards and cookies for the library staff who had helped them with their reading choices all year long. One year they made a card with a verse that read:

We have a sort of habit
To think of you when reading:
You know our likes and dislikes
And never are misleading.

So the first ones on our cookie list
When Christmas time draws near
Are all you girls who wait on us—

OUR FRIENDS SO VERY DEER!

Gertrude liked celebrations and occasions. They gave her a chance to share her spirit of fun. When some young friends came to visit her during a summer holiday at the Connecticut shore, she surprised them by putting on a wig and mimicking the popular Beatles singing group! Frances's husband, Mayo Hersey, said of Gertrude, she "is invariably the life of the party."

Gertrude Chandler Warner continued teaching, even when she was no longer standing in front of a classroom. In the 1950s, when she lived in a house with a big round front porch on Wilkinson and Grove Streets, she invited neighborhood children to sit beside her as she pointed out the constellations in the night sky.

In the 1960s and 1970s, children came to visit Gertrude in her house on Ring Street as soon as they finished one of her new books. Because Gertrude did not find it as easy to get around in her later years, the house had an elevator. The children got to ride upstairs in the elevator—and to discuss the book they had just read with its author.

Even when Gertrude was in her eighties, she invited children from the Putnam School to visit her. They came four at a time to have lemonade and to talk about books.

Gertrude was often doing generous things, and she always remembered to say thanks to others who were thoughtful.

For example, one little girl found a letter to Gertrude which had accidently dropped onto the street. The little girl, whose name was Tracy, brought the letter to Gertrude.

Tracy got this letter back from the author.

Dear Tracy—

You were a good little girl to return my letter, and I do thank you. It happened to be an important letter and it would have caused a lot of bother if it had been lost.

I am sending you the Caboose Mystery *in appreciation, and hope you will enjoy it. I should say it was just about your age and maybe older.*
Most sincerely,
— Gertrude C. Warner

When she was eighty-four, Gertrude shattered her right hip, and she could not walk very well after that. But she still enjoyed drives through the hills and valleys of northeastern Connecticut, and she still liked visiting with the people who meant a lot to her. In these years she could not see well enough to read much. But she listened to Talking Book records, so she was able to keep up with the books she had loved all her life. She also some-times watched television. She continued to write until her final illness, and to enjoy the letters she received from her readers. The children's letters, she said, were her "prop and stay."

In 1978 the library in the new Putnam Elementary School was named the Gertrude C. Warner Library, to honor Gertrude's interest in the young people of the area. Several hundred students gathered for the dedication. Although Gertrude was unable to attend, the ceremony was videotaped for her later viewing. The speaker said that naming the library was like completing a cycle; Gertrude had begun teaching sixty years earlier. He added, "Truly, she leaves footprints on the sands of time."

Gertrude Chandler Warner, in a funny way, had a lucky life. At one time or another, she broke her back, both hips, three or four ribs, and her knee. She had severe sore throats, had her tonsils removed twice, and her appendix once. She spent a lot of time at home recovering—and writing. It was her frequent ill health that gave her the time to do the writing which made her so well-known and successful.

In summing up her life, Gertrude said, "Remember the verse, 'the bruised reed He shall not break, and the smoking flax He shall not quench.' Well, in spite of disasters, I have never been entirely put out." Gertrude was pleased that despite all her illnesses and mishaps, she was able to do good work.

Gertrude Chandler Warner died in Putnam on August 30,

1979, after a long illness. She was eighty-nine years old. Later, the Congregational church in Putnam published in their newsletter, the *Beacon*, "Sunday School Lessons for Shut-Ins." These were two introductory chapters and four lessons which Gertrude had written for publication, although she had never completed the series. The *Beacon* noted, "We continue to feel Gertrude's presence among us and to profit by it—as we have for so long."

The marker at Gertrude's grave reads, "She opens her mouth with wisdom and the teaching of kindness is on her tongue."

Afterword

IN THE PUTNAM PUBLIC LIBRARY, high atop one of the shelving units, a miniature wooden boxcar rests. Below it, many copies of the first nineteen Boxcar mysteries line the shelves—or at least the copies that are not going home in a student's bookbag or are not already lying by a child's bedside, ready for a night's reading.

Some people in Putnam hope to buy a real boxcar or caboose and open a Gertrude Chandler Warner Museum. Then people can come from all over the world to visit the place where one of their favorite authors grew up. There they will see the books Gertrude published, her drawings and silhouettes, and the decorated holiday eggs she made for her students. The people of Putnam even have a copy of the dictionary Gertrude used for many years.

When grandparents in Putnam, Connecticut, tell their grandchildren about knowing Gertrude Chandler Warner, they tell them of her sense of fun, her imagination, and her kindliness. Most of all, they tell them how she could make all children who were in her classes or who read her books feel so good that they felt "ten feet tall"!

Today millions of young people from all over the world get to experience feeling "ten feet tall" as they continue to read the Boxcar books. Although Gertrude died in 1979, Boxcar Children Mysteries® are still being written. New authors take Henry, Jessie, Violet, and Benny on many new and different adventures.

The children work hard and enjoy themselves, are kind and thoughtful, visit interesting new places, and solve strange mysteries—just as they always have. And young readers get to go along for the ride. Gertrude Chandler Warner's imagination and energy still make the stories come alive.

The Publications of Gertrude Chandler Warner

THE BOXCAR CHILDREN MYSTERIES®

The Boxcar Children. Chicago: Scott, Foresman, 1942.

Surprise Island. Chicago: Scott, Foresman, 1949.

The Yellow House Mystery. Chicago: Albert Whitman, 1953.

Mystery Ranch. Chicago: Albert Whitman, 1958.

Mike's Mystery. Chicago: Albert Whitman, 1960.

Blue Bay Mystery. Chicago: Albert Whitman, 1961.

The Woodshed Mystery. Chicago: Albert Whitman, 1962.

The Lighthouse Mystery. Chicago: Albert Whitman, 1963.

Mountain Top Mystery. Chicago: Albert Whitman, 1964.

Schoolhouse Mystery. Chicago: Albert Whitman, 1965.

Caboose Mystery. Chicago: Albert Whitman, 1966.

Houseboat Mystery. Chicago: Albert Whitman, 1967.

Snowbound Mystery. Chicago: Albert Whitman, 1968.

Treehouse Mystery. Chicago: Albert Whitman, 1969.

Bicycle Mystery. Chicago: Albert Whitman, 1970.

Mystery in the Sand. Chicago: Albert Whitman, 1971.

Mystery Behind the Wall. Chicago: Albert Whitman, 1973.

Bus Station Mystery. Chicago: Albert Whitman, 1974.

Benny Uncovers a Mystery. Chicago: Albert Whitman, 1976.

OTHER CHILDREN'S BOOKS

The House of Delight. Boston: Pilgrim Press, 1916.

Star Stories for Little Folks. Boston: Pilgrim Press, 1918.

The Boxcar Children. Chicago: Rand McNally, 1924
     (with pictures by Dorothy Lake Gregory).

Good Americans: First Lessons in Citizenship; First Lessons for the Littlest Ones.
     Boston: Educational Publishing Company, 1926.

The World in a Barn. New York: Friendship Press, 1927.

Windows into Alaska. New York: Friendship Press, 1928.

The World on a Farm. New York: Friendship Press, 1931.

The Friendly Farmers. New York: Friendship Press, 1931 (with Elizabeth Harris).

Children of the Harvest. New York: Friendship Press, 1940.

Star Stories. Boston: Pilgrim Press, 1947.

1001 Nights. Chicago: Scott, Foresman, 1954.

Peter Piper: Missionary Parakeet. Grand Rapids, Mich.: Zondervan, 1967.

Adult Books

Life's Minor Collisions. Boston: Houghton Mifflin, 1921
    (with Frances Lester Warner).

Pleasures and Palaces. Boston: Houghton Mifflin, 1933
    (with Frances Lester Warner).

Henry Barnard. Hartford, Conn.: Connecticut State Teachers'
    Association, 1937 (with R. C. Jenkins).

History of Connecticut. Hartford, Conn.:
    Connecticut State Teachers' Association, 1948.

Sources

Albert Whitman & Company, Morton Grove, Illinois. Several pages of
  autobiographical material, and various articles.

Aspinock Historical Society, Putnam, Connecticut. Holdings: newspaper files,
  local histories, photographic records, and Gertrude Chandler Warner
  Reminiscences, 1972.

Brumbaugh, Mary. Library director, Putnam Public Library, 1996.
  Copies of thank-you notes from Warner and Welles to library staff.

Child, Mary. "Family Reminiscences," 1996.

Devlin, Jo Ellen. Children's librarian, Putnam Public Library.
  Conversations with author, 1991, 1992.

Dorman, Janet English. Student in Gertrude Warner's class and niece of
  Esther Welles. "Reminiscences," 1996.

Evans, Ray. "A Few Reflections I Have about Gertrude Warner," 1992, 1996.

Flagg, Ruth. Student in Gertrude Warner's first-grade class. Owner of silhouette.
  Conversation with author, 1996.

Flight, Vera. "Student Reminiscences," 1994.

Franklin, Isabel. Former teacher, Putnam Elementary School.
  Conversations with author, 1992, 1996.

Huss, Ruth. "Church Reminiscences," 1996.

Miller, Robert. Past President of the Aspinock Historical Society, Putnam,
  Connecticut. Loan of some early Gertrude Chandler Warner editions,
  photographs, and conversations with author, 1992, 1996.

Mistark, Tracy Stone. Owner of thank-you note. Conversation with author, 1993.

Neal, Courtney. Student researcher, Putnam High School, 1992.

Noonan, Betty. "Family Reminiscences and Mementos," 1996.

Pempack, Louise. "Reminiscences," 1996.

Putnam Patriot. Articles on Miss Warner and other family members, various dates.

Putnam Public Library. Gertrude Chandler Warner manuscript collection. Colleen Wittemore's reference and teaching materials.

Putnam Town Directories, 1888-1964. Putnam Public Library and Aspinock Historical Society.

Rubin, Caroline. "An Editor's Reminiscences," 1996.

Shaw, Mrs. Kevin. "Neighborhood Reminiscences," 1992.

Snow, Edith W. "Family Reminiscences," 1996.

Spooner, Earl. Owner of the Gertrude Chandler Home on South Main Street. Information on the Chandler home, 1995, 1996.

Warner, Frances. Endicott and I. Boston: Houghton Mifflin, 1919.

————. *Groups and Couples.* Boston: Riverside Press, 1923.

Warner, Gertrude Chandler. "Centennial Souvenir: 1848-1948: The Congregational Church, Putnam." Putnam, Conn. Chase Printery, 1948.

————. "A Sunday Afternoon Ride in 1898 and Thereafter," in *Perspectives of Putnam.* Edited by Margaret M. Weaver. Putnam, Conn. Wimco Printing, 1980, pp. 63-9.

Weaver, Margaret M. "Reminiscences," 1996.

Wittemore, Colleen. Classroom teacher, Putnam Elementary School. Owner of reference and teaching materials on Gertrude Chandler Warner. Conversations with author, 1991.

Ziegler, Jan. "Her *Boxcar Children* Delight Young Readers." *Courier, Norwich Bulletin*, April 19, 1977, pp. 4, 12.

ACKNOWLEDGMENTS

Any book requires the interest and support of numerous institutions and individuals. I wish to thank, in particular:

The many townspeople of Putnam and the surrounding area who shared reminiscences and artifacts.

The Aspinock Historical Society and the Putnam Public Library, who have encouraged the project by their generous sharing of information.

Robert Miller, past President of the Aspinock Historical Society, who has always been more than ready to seek answers to questions and to provide references.

Gertrude Chandler Warner's family members, Betty and Jim Noonan, who have also graciously shared both their interest and relevant materials.

And finally, Kathy Tucker and Christine Grant of Albert Whitman & Company, who have been thoughtful and careful editors.

—*Mary Ellen Ellsworth*

PHOTO CREDITS

INDEX

Numerals in italic type indicate photographs or illustrations.

Index

Index

INDEX

illness of, 9, 18, 58
and music, 18, 26, 43, 47, *48*
publicity work of, 23, 49
reading, 9, 57
retirement, 47
teaching, 23, 24-33, *29, 31, 33*, 42, 55
and trains, 7, 11, 15, *16*, 17, 53
traveling, 43-44, 55
volunteer work, 24, 26, 46-49, *48*, 53
work in publishing, 44
writing, 9-11, 21-22, 24-26, 42-47, *45*, 49-51, 53-54, 57
Warner, Ichabod, 8
Warner, Jane (Jennie) Elizabeth Carpenter (mother), 8-10, 18, 21-22, 24, 41-42
Warner, John (brother), 8-9, 12, *13*, 14-15, *16*, 17-19, 21-22, *34*, 42, 43
Welles, Esther, *38*, 49, 52, 54
Windham County, Connecticut, 8
Windows into Alaska, 42, 64
Woman of the Year Award, 53
Woodshed Mystery, 50, 63
Woodstock, Connecticut, 8, 12
World in a Barn, The, 42-43, 64
World on a Farm, The, 42-43, 64
World War I, 22-23

Yale University, 44
Yellow House Mystery, The, 50, 63
YWCA, 44